ALTO SAXOPHONE

TONS of TUNES

FOR THE HOLIDAYS

AMY ADAM
MIKE HANNICKEL

Edition Number: CMP 0693-02-400

Amy Adam, Mike Hannickel

TONS OF TUNES for the Holidays

Alto Saxophone

ISBN 978-90-431-1687-9

CD number: 19-027-3 CMP

CD arrangements by James L. Hosay

ARRANGERS

MIKE HANNICKEL grew up in the Sacramento, California area and attended California State University, Sacramento and the University of Southern California. He has been a music teacher in Rocklin, California since 1973. He also composes and publishes exclusively with Curnow Music Press with whom he has dozens of pieces of music in print.

AMY ADAM was raised in Grand Rapids, Minnesota and attended the University of Minnesota, Duluth graduating with a BM in band education and Flute performance. She has been a music teacher in California since 1992 and currently teaches in Rocklin, California.

TONS OF TUNES

TONS OF TUNES FOR THE HOLIDAYS is filled with the fun and familiar tunes that beginners love to play. All the songs have been arranged in keys that beginning band students learn in every popular band method. All **TONS OF TUNES FOR THE HOLIDAYS** books can be used together.

The **professional quality accompaniment CD** can be used for practice and performance. You may also choose to purchase the separately available Piano accompaniment part.

The songs are in **carefully graded** order. You will find appropriate music for every level of early beginner.

TO THE TEACHER:

For private studio teachers: **TONS OF TUNES FOR THE HOLIDAYS** is an excellent and versatile choice for use in those early recitals. You can also encourage your students to put on concerts at home for friends and family using the included CD.

For band directors: Motivate your students with these fun and easy songs! **TONS OF TUNES FOR THE HOLIDAYS** is designed so that any group of band instruments can play together. If, for instance, you have a beginning Flute, Alto Saxophone and Tuba player who would like to perform a piece together, you'll find what you need in this series.

Spotlight deserving young players in concert by including music featuring a soloist or small group. This also gives the band some needed rest.

TO THE MUSICIAN:

Have **FUN** playing these songs alone or with your friends! Even if you have different instruments, you can still play together. Each person needs to get the **TONS OF TUNES FOR THE HOLIDAYS** book for their instrument.

FOR THE HOLIDAYS

CONTENTS

TONS OF TUNES
FOR THE HOLIDAYS

ALTO SAXOPHONE

Amy Adam and
Mike Hannickel (ASCAP)

1. Jingle Bells

2. Jolly Old St. Nicholas

3. Up On the House Top

4. The Dreydl Song

5. O Come, Little Children

6. Good King Wenceslas

7. We Wish You a Merry Christmas

8. O Come All Ye Faithful

0693.02 CMP • Alto Saxophone

9. We Three Kings

TRACK 11

10. God Rest Ye Merry, Gentlemen

TRACK 12

11. Pat-A-Pan

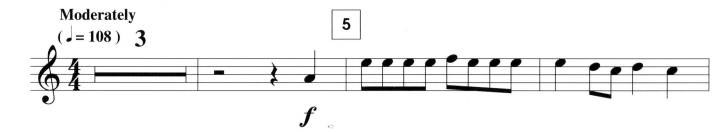

12. O Chanukah

   0693.02 CMP • Alto Saxophone

13. Silent Night

14. The Coventry Carol

11

15. Away in a Manger

16. O Christmas Tree

0693.02 CMP • Alto Saxophone

TRACK 19

17. Angels We Have Heard on High

TRACK 20

18. Bring a Torch, Jeanette, Isabella

19. Deck the Halls

Quick and lively
(♩ = 124)

20. Oh Little Town of Bethlehem

Slowly
(♩ = 86)

 0693.02 CMP • Alto Saxophone

21. Hark, the Herald Angels Sing

22. It Came Upon a Midnight Clear

23. Joy to the World

24. The First Noel

0693.02 CMP • Alto Saxophone

25. Toyland

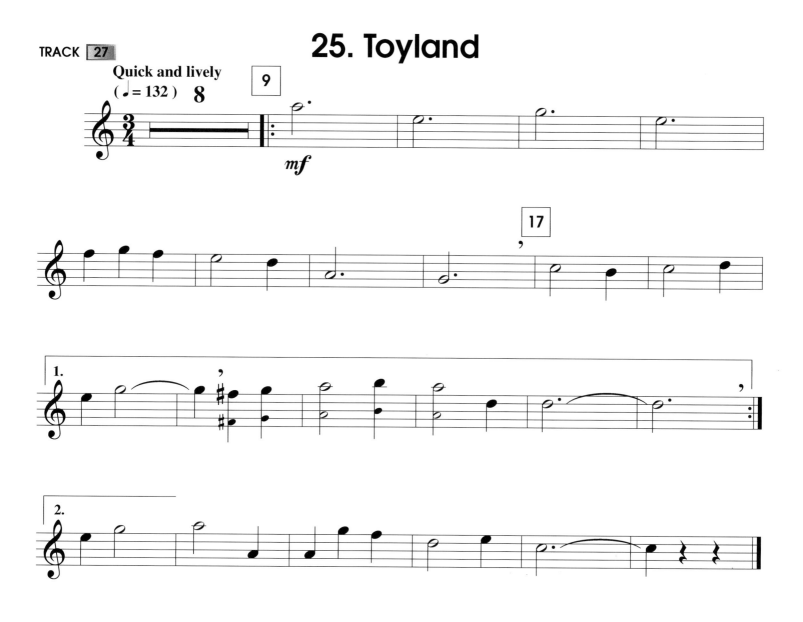

26. I Heard the Bells on Christmas Day

27. We Gather Together

28. Over the River

0693.02 CMP • Alto Saxophone

29. What Child is This?

30. Overture from the Nutckracker

31. Dance of the Sugar-Plum Fairy

32. Auld Lang Syne